NEW YORK

SHOPPING GUIDE 2024

A FRIENDLY GUIDE TO THE BEST SHOPPING IN THE CITY

EMILY R. PATEL

NEW YORK SHOPPING GUIDE 2024
Discover the best shopping destinations and
insider tips for a memorable experience.

© Emily R. Patel
© E.G.P. Editorial

ISBN-13: 9798853356382

INDEX

INTRODUCTION

This New York guide will help to discover the best shopping destinations and insider tips for a memorable experience.

The book includes a wide variety of stores ranging from high-end luxury boutiques to quirky independent shops, as well as markets and department stores.

The guide lists addresses, telephones, opening hours, information for tourists, curiosities, facts, how to get to each place and the attractions that are nearby.

New York Shopping Guide 2024 is an excellent companion for anyone looking to discover the best shopping experiences that New York has to offer.

SOUVENIR STORES

I LOVE NY BY
PHANTOM OF BROADWAY

Address: 1450 Broadway, New York, NY 10018.

Telephone: (212) 921-9070.

Monday-Saturday 9am-8pm, Sunday 10am-7pm.

Tourist information: I Love NY by Phantom Of Broadway is a souvenir and gift shop located in the heart of Times Square. It offers a variety of Broadway-themed items, including T-shirts, mugs, posters, and other memorabilia.

Curiosity and facts: The shop is named after the famous Broadway musical "The Phantom of the Opera," which has been running for over 30 years.

Getting there: The shop is located in the Times Square area, which is easily accessible by subway, bus, or taxi.

Nearby attractions: Times Square, the Broadway Theater District, Rockefeller Center.

GRAND SLAM NEW YORK

Address: 1557 Broadway,
New York, NY 10036.

Telephone: (212) 382-1155.

Monday-Saturday 9am-10pm, Sunday 10am-9pm.

Tourist information: Grand Slam New York is a souvenir and gift shop located in Times Square. It offers a wide range of New York-themed products, including clothing, accessories, and souvenirs.

Curiosity and facts: The shop has been featured in several TV shows and movies, including "Sex and the City" and "Spider-Man."

Getting there: The shop is located in the heart of Times Square, making it easily accessible by subway, bus, or taxi.

Nearby attractions: Times Square, the Broadway Theater District, Rockefeller Center.

MEMORIES OF NEW YORK

Address: 206B W 80th St,
New York, NY 10024.

Telephone: (212) 580-3922.

Monday-Saturday 10am-6pm, Sunday 11am-5pm.

Tourist information: Memories of New York is a small souvenir shop located on the Upper West Side. It offers a variety of New York-themed products, including postcards, magnets, keychains, and T-shirts.

Curiosity and facts: The shop has been serving customers for over 40 years and has become a neighborhood staple for both locals and tourists.

Getting there: The shop is located on the Upper West Side, near Central Park and the American Museum of Natural History. It can be easily reached by subway or bus.

Nearby attractions: Central Park, American Museum of Natural History, Lincoln Center.

CITYSTORE

Address: 1 Centre St,
New York, NY 10007.

Telephone: (212) 669-7553.

Monday-Friday 9am-5pm.

Tourist information: CityStore is the official gift shop of the City of New York. It offers a variety of New York-themed products, including books, apparel, and souvenirs.

Curiosity and facts: The shop is located inside the historic Municipal Building, which was completed in 1914 and served as the city's primary government building until the construction of City Hall.

Getting there: The shop is located in Lower Manhattan, near City Hall and the Brooklyn Bridge. It can be easily reached by subway or bus.

Nearby attractions: City Hall, Brooklyn Bridge, One World Trade Center.

THE STATUE OF LIBERTY GIFT SHOP

Address: Liberty Island,
New York, NY 10004.

Telephone: (212) 561-4500.

Monday-Sunday 8:30am-6:30pm.

Tourist information: The Statue of Liberty Gift Shop is located on Liberty Island and offers a variety of Statue of Liberty-themed products, including replicas, postcards, and T-shirts.

Curiosity and facts: The Statue of Liberty was a gift from France to the United States in 1886 and has since become a symbol of freedom and democracy.

Getting there: Visitors must take a ferry to Liberty Island from Battery Park in Lower Manhattan. The gift shop is located near the statue.

Nearby attractions: Ellis Island, One World Trade Center, Battery Park.

NY GIFTS

Address: 301 Park Ave, New York, NY 10022.

Telephone: (212) 888-1188.

Monday-Saturday 9am-7pm, Sunday 10am-6pm.

Tourist information: NY Gifts is a souvenir and gift shop located near Grand Central Terminal. It offers a variety of New York-themed products, including apparel, accessories, and postcards.

Curiosity and facts: The shop has been serving customers for over 20 years and has become a popular destination for tourists and locals alike.

Getting there: The shop is located near Grand Central Terminal, making it easily accessible by subway, train, or bus.

Nearby attractions: Grand Central Terminal, Bryant Park, Rockefeller Center.

THE NEW YORK CITY STORE

Address: 314 Fifth Ave,
New York, NY 10001.

Telephone: (212) 868-1571.

Monday-Saturday 10am-8pm, Sunday 11am-7pm.

Tourist information: The New York City Store is a souvenir and gift shop located near the Empire State Building. It offers a variety of New York-themed products, including T-shirts, mugs, and postcards.

Curiosity and facts: The shop has been featured in several TV shows and movies, including "Friends" and "How I Met Your Mother."

Getting there: The shop is located near the Empire State Building, making it easily accessible by subway, bus, or taxi.

Nearby attractions: Empire State Building, Madison Square Garden, Herald Square.

THE 9/11 MEMORIAL & MUSEUM STORE

Address: 180 Greenwich St,
New York, NY 10007.

Telephone: (212) 312-8800.

Monday-Sunday 9am-8pm.

Tourist information: The 9/11 Memorial & Museum Store is located near the World Trade Center site and offers a variety of commemorative items related to the events of September 11, 2001.

Curiosity and facts: The store is part of the 9/11 Memorial & Museum, which was built to honor the victims of the attacks and educate visitors about the events of that day.

Getting there: The store is located near the World Trade Center site, making it easily accessible by subway, train, or bus.

Nearby attractions: 9/11 Memorial & Museum, One World Trade Center, Battery Park.

THE EMPIRE STATE BUILDING OFFICIAL GIFT SHOP

Address: 350 Fifth Ave,
New York, NY 10118.

Telephone: (212) 736-3100.

Monday-Sunday 8am-2am.

Tourist information: The Empire State Building Official Gift Shop is located inside the iconic Empire State Building and offers a variety of New York-themed products, including T-shirts, mugs, and keychains.

Curiosity and facts: The Empire State Building was completed in 1931 and was the tallest building in the world until the construction of the World Trade Center in 1972.

Getting there: The gift shop is located inside the Empire State Building, which is easily accessible by subway, train, or bus.

Nearby attractions: Empire State Building, Madison Square Garden, Herald Square.

TIMES SQUARE
GIFTS & SOUVENIRS

Address: 1567 Broadway,
New York, NY 10036.

Telephone: (212) 869-3544.

Monday-Sunday 9am-11pm.

Tourist information: Times Square Gifts & Souvenirs is a souvenir and gift shop located in the heart of Times Square. It offers a wide range of New York-themed products, including clothing, accessories, and postcards.

Curiosity and facts: Times Square is one of the busiest tourist destinations in the world and is known for its bright lights, billboards, and bustling crowds.

Getting there: The shop is located in the heart of Times Square, making it easily accessible by subway, bus, or taxi.

Nearby attractions: Times Square, the Broadway Theater District, Rockefeller Center.

CLOTHING STORES

MACY'S HERALD SQUARE

Address: 151 W 34th St,
New York, NY 10001.

Telephone: +1 212-695-4400.

Mon-Sat: 10AM-9PM, Sun: 11AM-8PM.

Tourist information: Macy's Herald Square is the flagship store of the Macy's department store chain and is located in Midtown Manhattan. It is a must-visit for shoppers and tourists alike, with over 1.1 million square feet of retail space spread over 10 floors.

Curiosity and facts: The store was opened in 1902 and was the first building in the world to have a modern-day escalator. It also hosts the annual Macy's Thanksgiving Day Parade, which attracts millions of visitors each year.

Getting there: Macy's Herald Square is easily accessible by subway, with several lines stopping nearby. The store is also within walking distance of Penn Station and the Port Authority Bus Terminal.

Nearby attractions: Macy's Herald Square is located in the heart of Midtown Manhattan, with many other famous attractions nearby, such as the Empire State Building and Madison Square Garden.

BLOOMINGDALE'S

Address: 1000 Third Avenue, New York, NY 10022.

Telephone: +1 212-705-2000.

Mon-Sat: 10AM-9PM, Sun: 11AM-7PM.

Tourist information: Bloomingdale's is a luxury department store located on the Upper East Side of Manhattan. It is known for its designer fashion, beauty products, and home goods.

Curiosity and facts: The store was opened in 1872 and has since expanded to locations across the United States. It is a popular shopping destination for both locals and tourists, with its iconic brown bags and signature "Big Brown Bear" mascot.

Getting there: Bloomingdale's is easily accessible by subway, with several lines stopping nearby. The store is also within walking distance of Central Park and the Metropolitan Museum of Art.

Nearby attractions: Bloomingdale's is located on the Upper East Side of Manhattan, with many other upscale shops and restaurants nearby. The Metropolitan Museum of Art and Central Park are also within walking distance.

SAKS FIFTH AVENUE

Address: 611 Fifth Avenue,
New York, NY 10022.

Telephone: +1 212-753-4000.

Mon-Sat: 10AM-8:30PM, Sun: 11AM-7PM.

Tourist information: Saks Fifth Avenue is a luxury department store located on Fifth Avenue in Midtown Manhattan. It is known for its high-end fashion, jewelry, and beauty products.

Curiosity and facts: The store was opened in 1924 and has since become a landmark of New York City. It is famous for its elaborate holiday window displays, which attract crowds of tourists each year.

Getting there: Saks Fifth Avenue is easily accessible by subway, with several lines stopping nearby. The store is also within walking distance of Rockefeller Center and St. Patrick's Cathedral.

Nearby attractions: Saks Fifth Avenue is located on Fifth Avenue in Midtown Manhattan, with many other high-end shops and restaurants nearby. Rockefeller Center and St. Patrick's Cathedral are also within walking distance.

CENTURY 21

Address: 22 Cortlandt Street, New York, NY 10007.

Telephone: +1 212-227-9092.

Mon-Sat: 10AM-9PM, Sun: 11AM-8PM.

Tourist information: Century 21 is a discount department store located in Lower Manhattan. It offers a wide range of fashion, beauty, and home goods at discounted prices.

Curiosity and facts: The store was opened in 1961 and has since become a popular shopping destination for bargain hunters. It is also known for its "grab bags," which are filled with surprise items and sold at a discounted price.

Getting there: Century 21 is easily accessible by subway, with several lines stopping nearby. The store is also within walking distance of the World Trade Center and the 9/11 Memorial.

Nearby attractions: Century 21 is located in Lower Manhattan, with many other shops, restaurants, and attractions nearby. The World Trade Center and the 9/11 Memorial are also within walking distance.

BERGDORF GOODMAN

Address: 754 Fifth Avenue,
New York, NY 10019.

Telephone: +1 212-753-7300.

Mon-Sat: 10AM-7PM, Sun: 12PM-6PM.

Tourist information: Bergdorf Goodman is a luxury department store located on Fifth Avenue in Midtown Manhattan. It is known for its high-end fashion, jewelry, and home goods.

Curiosity and facts: The store was opened in 1901 and has since become a landmark of New York City. It is famous for its elaborate window displays, which are designed by some of the most renowned designers in the world.

Getting there: Bergdorf Goodman is easily accessible by subway, with several lines stopping nearby. The store is also within walking distance of Central Park and the Museum of Modern Art.

Nearby attractions: Bergdorf Goodman is located on Fifth Avenue in Midtown Manhattan, with many other high-end shops and restaurants nearby. Central Park and the Museum of Modern Art are also within walking distance.

UNIQLO

Address: 666 Fifth Avenue, New York, NY 10103.

Telephone: +1 877-486-4756.

Mon-Sat: 10AM-8PM, Sun: 11AM-7PM.

Tourist information: Uniqlo is a Japanese clothing brand that offers affordable fashion for men, women, and children. Its flagship store in New York City is located on Fifth Avenue in Midtown Manhattan.

Curiosity and facts: The store was opened in 2011 and has since become a popular shopping destination for those looking for stylish and affordable clothing. Uniqlo is also known for its innovative clothing technologies, such as its HEATTECH line.

Getting there: Uniqlo is easily accessible by subway, with several lines stopping nearby. The store is also within walking distance of Rockefeller Center and St. Patrick's Cathedral.

Nearby attractions: Uniqlo is located on Fifth Avenue in Midtown Manhattan, with many other shops, restaurants, and attractions nearby. Rockefeller Center and St. Patrick's Cathedral are also within walking distance.

ZARA

Address: 503 Broadway,
New York, NY 10012.

Telephone: +1 212-343-1725.

Mon-Sat: 10AM-9PM, Sun: 11AM-8PM.

Tourist information: Zara is a Spanish clothing brand that offers affordable and stylish fashion for men, women, and children. Its flagship store in New York City is located in SoHo.

Curiosity and facts: The store was opened in 2011 and has since become a popular shopping destination for those looking for trendy and affordable clothing. Zara is also known for its fast-fashion business model, which allows it to quickly adapt to changing fashion trends.

Getting there: Zara is easily accessible by subway, with several lines stopping nearby. The store is also within walking distance of many other shops, restaurants, and attractions in SoHo.

Nearby attractions: Zara is located in SoHo, which is known for its trendy shops, restaurants, and art galleries. The area is also home to several historic buildings and landmarks.

H&M

Address: 435 Seventh Avenue, New York, NY 10001.

Telephone: +1 855-466-7467.

Mon-Sat: 10AM-9PM, Sun: 11AM-8PM.

Tourist information: H&M is a Swedish clothing brand that offers affordable and stylish fashion for men, women, and children. Its flagship store in New York City is located in Midtown Manhattan.

Curiosity and facts: The store was opened in 2000 and has since become a popular shopping destination for those looking for trendy and affordable clothing. H&M is also known for its collaborations with famous designers and celebrities.

Getting there: H&M is easily accessible by subway, with several lines stopping nearby. The store is also within walking distance of the Empire State Building and Madison Square Garden.

Nearby attractions: H&M is located in Midtown Manhattan, with many other shops, restaurants, and attractions nearby. The Empire State Building and Madison Square Garden are also within walking distance.

TOPSHOP

Address: 608 Fifth Avenue,
New York, NY 10020.

Telephone: +1 212-757-8240.

Mon-Sat: 10AM-9PM, Sun: 11AM-8PM.

Tourist information: Topshop is a British clothing brand that offers affordable and trendy fashion for women. Its flagship store in New York City is located on Fifth Avenue in Midtown Manhattan.

Curiosity and facts: The store was opened in 2009 and has since become a popular shopping destination for fashion-forward women. Topshop is also known for its collaborations with famous designers and celebrities.

Getting there: Topshop is easily accessible by subway, with several lines stopping nearby. The store is also within walking distance of Rockefeller Center and St. Patrick's Cathedral.

Nearby attractions: Topshop is located on Fifth Avenue in Midtown Manhattan, with many other shops, restaurants, and attractions nearby. Rockefeller Center and St. Patrick's Cathedral are also within walking distance.

NORDSTROM

Address: 225 W 57th St,
New York, NY 10019.

Telephone: +1 646-952-2000.

Mon-Sat: 10AM-9PM, Sun: 11AM-7PM.

Tourist information: Nordstrom is a luxury department store chain that offers high-end fashion, beauty, and home goods. Its flagship store in New York City is located on 57th Street in Midtown Manhattan.

Curiosity and facts: The store was opened in 2019 and has since become a popular shopping destination for those looking for luxury products. Nordstrom is also known for its excellent customer service and its commitment to sustainability.

Getting there: Nordstrom is easily accessible by subway, with several lines stopping nearby. The store is also within walking distance of Central Park and the Museum of Modern Art.

Nearby attractions: Nordstrom is located on 57th Street in Midtown Manhattan, with many other high-end shops and restaurants nearby. Central Park and the Museum of Modern Art are also within walking distance.

JEWELRY STORES

TIFFANY & CO.

Address: 727 Fifth Ave,
New York, NY 10022, United States.

Telephone: +1 212-755-8000.

Mon-Sat: 10am-6pm, Sun: 12pm-5pm.

Tourist information: Tiffany & Co. is a world-renowned jeweler and specialty retailer, offering an array of timeless jewelry designs and luxury accessories. Founded in 1837, Tiffany & Co. has become a symbol of luxury and elegance, catering to the world's most discerning clientele. Visitors to the flagship store in New York City can explore a wide range of exquisite jewelry and unique gifts, including engagement rings, signature collections, and custom pieces crafted by master artisans.

Curiosity and facts: Tiffany & Co. is famous for designing the NFL's Vince Lombardi Trophy and creating the iconic blue box that has become synonymous with luxury and romance. Additionally, the store's windows are a popular attraction during the holiday season, featuring intricate holiday-themed displays.

Getting there: The flagship Tiffany & Co. store is located on Fifth Avenue in Midtown Manhattan, easily accessible by public transportation or taxi. Visitors can take the subway to the 5th Ave/59th St station (N, Q, R, W lines) or the 57th St station (F line), or hop on a bus that runs along Fifth Avenue.

Nearby attractions: The Tiffany & Co. flagship store is located near many other luxury retailers and iconic New York City landmarks, including Central Park, Rockefeller Center, and the Museum of Modern Art.

CARTIER

Address: 653 Fifth Ave,
New York, NY 10022, United States.

Telephone: +1 212-753-0111.

Mon-Sat: 10am-6pm, Sun: 12pm-5pm.

Tourist information: Cartier is a French luxury goods company that specializes in jewelry, watches, and fragrances. The flagship store in New York City is located on Fifth Avenue and showcases some of the brand's most iconic designs, including the Love bracelet and Trinity ring. Visitors can also explore a range of high-end watches, handbags, and accessories.

Curiosity and facts: Cartier has a long history of creating iconic pieces for royalty and celebrities, including Princess Grace of Monaco and Elizabeth Taylor. Additionally, the Cartier Mansion, located adjacent to the flagship store, is a historic landmark and popular venue for events and private parties.

Getting there: The Cartier flagship store is located on Fifth Avenue in Midtown Manhattan, easily accessible by public transportation or taxi. Visitors can take the subway to the 5th Ave/59th St station (N, Q, R, W lines) or the 57th St station (F line), or hop on a bus that runs along Fifth Avenue.

Nearby attractions: The Cartier flagship store is located near many other luxury retailers and iconic New York City landmarks, including Central Park, Rockefeller Center, and the Museum of Modern Art.

HARRY WINSTON

Address: 718 Fifth Ave,
New York, NY 10019, United States.

Telephone: +1 212-399-1000.

Mon-Sat: 10am-6pm, Sun: 12pm-5pm.

Tourist information: Harry Winston is a luxury jewelry and watch brand that has been synonymous with elegance and glamour for over eight decades. The flagship store in New York City offers a range of stunning pieces, from diamond necklaces and earrings to engagement rings and custom creations. Visitors can also explore the brand's exclusive high jewelry collection and limited edition timepieces.

Curiosity and facts: Harry Winston is famous for owning some of the world's most remarkable diamonds, including the Hope Diamond and the Lesotho Promise. Additionally, the brand has a long history of collaborating with Hollywood, providing jewelry for some of the biggest names in the entertainment industry.

Getting there: The Harry Winston flagship store is located on Fifth Avenue in Midtown Manhattan, easily accessible by public transportation or taxi. Visitors can take the subway to the 5th Ave/53rd St station (E, M lines) or the 57th St station (F line), or hop on a bus that runs along Fifth Avenue.

Nearby attractions: The Harry Winston flagship store is located near many other luxury retailers and iconic New York City landmarks, including Central Park,

Rockefeller Center, and the Museum of Modern Art.

DAVID YURMAN

Address: 712 Madison Ave,
New York, NY 10065, United States.

Telephone: +1 212-752-4255.

Mon-Sat: 10am-6pm, Sun: 12pm-5pm.

Tourist information: David Yurman is a luxury jewelry brand that combines contemporary design with traditional craftsmanship. The flagship store on Madison Avenue offers a range of timeless pieces, from the iconic Cable bracelet to diamond and gemstone jewelry. Visitors can also explore the brand's unique men's collection and wedding jewelry.

Curiosity and facts: David Yurman's signature Cable bracelet was inspired by the cables on a ship's rigging, and the brand has continued to draw inspiration from the sea in many of its designs. Additionally, David Yurman is committed to sustainability and sources materials responsibly, using recycled metals and ethically-sourced gemstones whenever possible.

Getting there: The David Yurman flagship store is located on Madison Avenue in the Upper East Side of Manhattan, easily accessible by public transportation or taxi. Visitors can take the subway to the 68th St/Hunter College station (6 line) or the 72nd St station (Q line), or hop on a bus that runs along Madison Avenue.

Nearby attractions: The David Yurman flagship store is located near many other luxury retailers and cultural attractions, including the Metropolitan Museum of Art and Central Park.

BVLGARI

Address: 730 Fifth Ave,
New York, NY 10019, United States.

Telephone: +1 212-315-9000.

Mon-Sat: 10am-6pm, Sun: 12pm-5pm.

Tourist information: Bvlgari is an Italian luxury brand that specializes in jewelry, watches, and accessories. The flagship store on Fifth Avenue showcases the brand's signature designs, including the iconic Serpenti collection and bold, colorful gemstone jewelry. Visitors can also explore the brand's exclusive high jewelry collection and limited edition timepieces.

Curiosity and facts: Bvlgari has a long history of collaborating with celebrities and artists, including Andy Warhol and Elizabeth Taylor. Additionally, the brand's heritage can be seen in its use of ancient Roman motifs and techniques in many of its designs.

Getting there: The Bvlgari flagship store is located on Fifth Avenue in Midtown Manhattan, easily accessible by public transportation or taxi. Visitors can take the subway to the 5th Ave/53rd St station (E, M lines) or the 57th St station (F line), or hop on a bus that runs along Fifth Avenue.

Nearby attractions: The Bvlgari flagship store is located near many other luxury retailers and iconic New York City landmarks, including Central Park, Rockefeller Center, and the Museum of Modern Art.

VAN CLEEF & ARPELS

Address: 744 Fifth Ave,
New York, NY 10019, United States.

Telephone: +1 212-826-2900.

Mon-Sat: 10am-6pm, Sun: 12pm-5pm.

Tourist information: Van Cleef & Arpels is a French luxury brand that specializes in jewelry and watches. The flagship store on Fifth Avenue features a range of elegant pieces, from delicate flower-inspired designs to the iconic Alhambra collection. Visitors can also explore the brand's exclusive high jewelry collection and limited edition timepieces.

Curiosity and facts: Van Cleef & Arpels is known for its use of innovative jewelry-making techniques, including the "Mystery Set" technique that creates the illusion of gemstones floating in the air. Additionally, the brand has a long history of collaborating with artists and designers, including Salvador Dali and Pierre Arpels.

Getting there: The Van Cleef & Arpels flagship store is located on Fifth Avenue in Midtown Manhattan, easily accessible by public transportation or taxi. Visitors can take the subway to the 5th Ave/53rd St station (E, M lines) or the 57th St station (F line), or hop on a bus that runs along Fifth Avenue.

Nearby attractions: The Van Cleef & Arpels flagship store is located near many other luxury retailers and iconic New York City landmarks, including Central Park, Rockefeller Center, and the Museum of Modern Art.

BUCCELLATI

Address: 714 Madison Ave,
New York, NY 10065, United States.

Telephone: +1 212-308-2900.

Mon-Sat: 10am-6pm, Sun: 12pm-5pm.

Tourist information: Buccellati is an Italian luxury brand that specializes in jewelry and silverware. The flagship store on Madison Avenue offers a range of stunning pieces, from delicate gold lacework to intricately designed silver serving pieces. Visitors can also explore the brand's limited edition jewelry collections and bespoke designs.

Curiosity and facts: Buccellati is known for its unique approach to jewelry-making, combining traditional techniques with innovative designs. Additionally, the brand has a long history of collaborating with artists and designers, including Salvador Dali and Alain Delon.

Getting there: The Buccellati flagship store is located on Madison Avenue in the Upper East Side of Manhattan, easily accessible by public transportation or taxi. Visitors can take the subway to the 68th St/Hunter College station (6 line) or the 72nd St station (Q line), or hop on a bus that runs along Madison Avenue.

Nearby attractions: The Buccellati flagship store is located near many other luxury retailers and cultural attractions, including the Metropolitan Museum of Art and Central Park.

CHOPARD

Address: 709 Madison Ave,
New York, NY 10065, United States.

Telephone: +1 212-223-2304.

Mon-Sat: 10am-6pm Sun: 12pm-5pm.

Tourist information: Chopard is a Swiss luxury brand that specializes in jewelry and watches. The flagship store on Madison Avenue offers a range of elegant pieces, from classic diamond necklaces to contemporary designs. Visitors can also explore the brand's limited edition jewelry collections and high-end timepieces.

Curiosity and facts: Chopard is known for its commitment to sustainability, using ethical sourcing and responsible manufacturing processes in its jewelry and watchmaking. Additionally, the brand has a long history of collaborating with the Cannes Film Festival, creating the iconic Palme d'Or trophy each year.

Getting there: The Chopard flagship store is located on Madison Avenue in the Upper East Side of Manhattan, easily accessible by public transportation or taxi. Visitors can take the subway to the 68th St/Hunter College station (6 line) or the 72nd St station (Q line), or hop on a bus that runs along Madison Avenue.

Nearby attractions: The Chopard flagship store is located near many other luxury retailers and cultural attractions, including the Metropolitan Museum of Art and Central Park.

ANNA SHEFFIELD

Address: 19 Bleecker St,
New York, NY 10012, United States.

Telephone: +1 212-925-7010.

Mon-Sat: 11am-7pm, Sun: 12pm-6pm.

Tourist information: Anna Sheffield is a contemporary jewelry brand that blends vintage-inspired designs with modern elements. The flagship store in NoLIta offers a range of unique pieces, from engagement rings and wedding bands to stackable rings and personalized jewelry. Visitors can also explore the brand's one-of-a-kind custom designs.

Curiosity and facts: Anna Sheffield's signature designs are inspired by nature, featuring organic shapes and delicate details. Additionally, the brand has a strong commitment to sustainability and uses recycled metals and ethically-sourced gemstones in its jewelry.

Getting there: The Anna Sheffield flagship store is located in NoLIta (North of Little Italy), easily accessible by public transportation or taxi. Visitors can take the subway to the Broadway-Lafayette St station (B, D, F, M lines) or the Spring St station (6 line), or hop on a bus that runs along Bowery or Lafayette St.

Nearby attractions: The Anna Sheffield flagship store is located near many trendy restaurants, cafes, and boutique shops in NoLIta, as well as cultural attractions such as the New Museum and the Lower East Side Tenement Museum.

CATBIRD

Address: 219 Bedford Ave, Brooklyn, NY 11211, United States.

Telephone: +1 718-599-3457.

Mon-Sat: 12pm-7pm, Sun: 12pm-6pm.

Tourist information: Catbird is a Brooklyn-based jewelry brand that offers a range of delicate and minimalistic pieces. The flagship store in Williamsburg features the brand's signature stackable rings, hoop earrings, and charm necklaces, as well as a curated selection of gifts and accessories from other independent designers.

Curiosity and facts: Catbird is committed to sustainability and ethical production, using recycled metals and conflict-free diamonds in its jewelry. Additionally, the brand has a strong focus on supporting local artisans and designers, featuring many handmade and one-of-a-kind pieces in its collections.

Getting there: The Catbird flagship store is located in Williamsburg, easily accessible by public transportation or taxi. Visitors can take the subway to the Bedford Ave station (L line) or the Metropolitan Ave station (G, L lines), or hop on a bus that runs along Bedford Ave.

Nearby attractions: The Catbird flagship store is located in the heart of Williamsburg, a trendy neighborhood with a vibrant arts and culture scene. Visitors can explore the many galleries, boutiques, and restaurants in the area, or take a stroll along the nearby East River waterfront.

DEPARTMENT STORES

MACY'S HERALD SQUARE

Address: 151 W 34th St, New York, NY 10001.

Telephone: (212) 695-4400.

Monday-Saturday 10am-9:30pm, Sunday 11am-8pm.

Tourist Information: Macy's Herald Square is the world's largest department store with over 1.1 million square feet of retail space.

Curiosity and Facts: The first Macy's Thanksgiving Day Parade was held in 1924 and featured live animals from the Central Park Zoo.

Getting There: Macy's Herald Square is easily accessible by subway and bus, located near the 34th Street/Herald Square station.

Nearby Attractions: Empire State Building, Madison Square Garden, Herald Square Park.

BLOOMINGDALE'S

Address: 1000 Third Avenue,
New York, NY 10022.

Telephone: (212) 705-2000.

Monday-Saturday 10am-9pm, Sunday 11am-8pm.

Tourist Information: Bloomingdale's is a luxury department store that offers a range of high-end fashion and home goods.

Curiosity and Facts: Bloomingdale's iconic "brown bag" was introduced in 1973 and has since become a symbol of the store's brand.

Getting There: Bloomingdale's is easily accessible by subway and bus, located near the 59th Street/Lexington Avenue station.

Nearby Attractions: Central Park, The Plaza Hotel, Museum Mile.

SAKS FIFTH AVENUE

Address: 611 Fifth Avenue,
New York, NY 10022.

Telephone: (212) 753-4000.

Monday-Saturday 10am-8pm, Sunday 11am-7pm.

Tourist Information: Saks Fifth Avenue is a luxury department store that offers a wide range of designer fashion and beauty products.

Curiosity and Facts: Saks Fifth Avenue's flagship store was opened in 1924 and has since become a landmark of New York City's Fifth Avenue shopping district.

Getting There: Saks Fifth Avenue is easily accessible by subway and bus, located near the 5th Avenue/53rd Street station.

Nearby Attractions: Rockefeller Center, St. Patrick's Cathedral, Museum of Modern Art.

BERGDORF GOODMAN

Address: 754 Fifth Avenue,
New York, NY 10019.

Telephone: (212) 753-7300.

Monday-Saturday 10am-8pm, Sunday 11am-7pm.

Tourist Information: Bergdorf Goodman is a luxury department store that offers a range of high-end fashion and home goods.

Curiosity and Facts: The store was founded in 1899 by Herman Bergdorf and was later purchased by Edwin Goodman in 1901, giving the store its current name.

Getting There: Bergdorf Goodman is easily accessible by subway and bus, located near the 5th Avenue/59th Street station.

Nearby Attractions: Central Park, The Plaza Hotel, Museum Mile.

NORDSTROM

Address: 225 Liberty Street, New York, NY 10281.

Telephone: (212) 295-2000.

Monday-Saturday 10am-9pm, Sunday 11am-7pm.

Tourist Information: Nordstrom is a luxury department store that offers a range of high-end fashion, beauty products, and home goods.

Curiosity and Facts: Nordstrom's first New York City location opened in 2019 and features a unique glass facade inspired by the city's iconic skyscrapers.

Getting There: Nordstrom is easily accessible by subway and bus, located near the World Trade Center station.

Nearby Attractions: One World Trade Center, 9/11 Memorial & Museum, Brookfield Place.

NEIMAN MARCUS

Address: 20 Hudson Yards,
New York, NY 10001.

Telephone: (646) 562-3500.

Monday-Saturday 10am-9pm, Sunday 11am-7pm.

Tourist Information: Neiman Marcus is a luxury department store that offers a range of high-end fashion, beauty products, and home goods.

Curiosity and Facts: The store's first New York City location opened in 2019 and features a futuristic design with a unique staircase that spirals up to the second floor.

Getting There: Neiman Marcus is easily accessible by subway and bus, located near the 34th Street/Hudson Yards station.

Nearby Attractions: The Vessel at Hudson Yards, High Line, Chelsea Market.

BARNEYS NEW YORK

Address: 660 Madison Avenue,
New York, NY 10065.

Telephone: (212) 826-8900.

Monday-Saturday 10am-7pm, Sunday 11am-6pm.

Tourist Information: Barneys New York is a luxury department store that offers a range of high-end fashion, beauty products, and home goods.

Curiosity and Facts: Barneys New York was founded in 1923 as a men's clothing store and later expanded to include women's fashion and home goods.

Getting There: Barneys New York is easily accessible by subway and bus, located near the 5th Avenue/59th Street station.

Nearby Attractions: Central Park, The Plaza Hotel, Museum Mile.

LORD & TAYLOR

Address: 424 Fifth Avenue,
New York, NY 10018.

Telephone: (212) 391-3344.

Monday-Saturday 10am-8pm, Sunday 11am-7pm.

Tourist Information: Lord & Taylor is a luxury department store that offers a range of high-end fashion and home goods.

Curiosity and Facts: Lord & Taylor's flagship store on Fifth Avenue was opened in 1914 and features a landmarked Italian Renaissance-style facade.

Getting There: Lord & Taylor is easily accessible by subway and bus, located near the 42nd Street/Bryant Park station.

Nearby Attractions: Bryant Park, New York Public Library, Empire State Building.

CENTURY 21

Address: 22 Cortlandt Street,
New York, NY 10007.

Telephone: (212) 227-9092.

Monday-Saturday 10am-8pm, Sunday 11am-7pm.

Tourist Information: Century 21 is a discount department store that offers a range of fashion, beauty products, and home goods at discounted prices.

Curiosity and Facts: Century 21's flagship store in Lower Manhattan was opened in 1961 and was one of the first stores in the area to offer discounted designer merchandise.

Getting There: Century 21 is easily accessible by subway and bus, located near the Cortlandt Street station.

Nearby Attractions: One World Trade Center, 9/11 Memorial & Museum, Battery Park.

TARGET

Address: 517 E 117th St,
New York, NY 10035.

Telephone: (212) 835-0860.

Monday-Saturday 8am-10pm, Sunday 8am-9pm.

Tourist Information: Target is a discount department store that offers a range of fashion, beauty products, and home goods at discounted prices.

Curiosity and Facts: Target's first small-format store in Manhattan opened in 2018 and offers a unique shopping experience for city residents.

Getting There: Target is easily accessible by subway and bus, located near the 116th Street station.

Nearby Attractions: Museum of the City of New York, Central Park, Marcus Garvey Park.

BOOKSTORES
STORES

STRAND BOOKSTORE

Address: 828 Broadway,
New York, NY 10003, United States.

Telephone: +1 212-473-1452.

Monday - Sunday: 10:00 AM - 10:30 PM.

Tourist information: The Strand is one of the largest independent bookstores in the world, with over 2.5 million new, used, and rare books in stock. Founded in 1927, it has become a cultural icon and a must-visit destination for book lovers.

Curiosity and facts: The Strand was originally located on Fourth Avenue, known as "Book Row," which was once home to 48 bookstores. The Strand's famous slogan, "18 Miles of Books," refers to the total length of its bookshelves.

Getting there: The Strand is located in the East Village neighborhood of Manhattan, easily accessible by subway (N, Q, R, W, 4, 5, 6, and L trains).

Nearby Attractions: Union Square Park, Washington Square Park, New York University, and Cooper Union.

MCNALLY JACKSON

Address: 52 Prince St,
New York, NY 10012, United States.

Telephone: +1 212-274-1160.

Monday - Sunday: 10:00 AM - 9:00 PM.

Tourist information: McNally Jackson is an independent bookstore and publisher located in the heart of SoHo. With a carefully curated selection of books, a cozy atmosphere, and a cafe, it's a great place to spend an afternoon.

Curiosity and facts: McNally Jackson has an Espresso Book Machine, which prints and binds books on demand. They also host a variety of literary events, including author readings, book clubs, and writing workshops.

Getting there: McNally Jackson is located in the SoHo neighborhood of Manhattan, easily accessible by subway (N, Q, R, W, 4, 5, 6, and B, D, F, and M trains).

Nearby Attractions: The New Museum, The Drawing Center, and the iconic SoHo cast-iron buildings.

THREE LIVES & COMPANY

Address: 154 W 10th St,
New York, NY 10014, United States.

Telephone: +1 212-741-2069.

Monday - Saturday: 12:00 PM - 7:00 PM,
Sunday: 12:00 PM - 6:00 PM.

Tourist information: Three Lives & Company is a cozy neighborhood bookstore in the West Village. With a well-curated selection of new and classic titles, it's a great place to browse and discover new reads.

Curiosity and facts: The store was named after a novel by Gertrude Stein. It was founded in 1978 and has been a neighborhood institution ever since.

Getting there: Three Lives & Company is located in the West Village neighborhood of Manhattan, easily accessible by subway (A, C, E, B, D, F, and M trains).

Nearby Attractions: The High Line, the Whitney Museum of American Art, and the Meatpacking District.

BOOKS ARE MAGIC

Address: 225 Smith St, Brooklyn,
NY 11231, United States.

Telephone: +1 718-246-2665.

Monday - Sunday: 10:00 AM - 7:00 PM.

Tourist information: Books Are Magic is an independent bookstore in the heart of Brooklyn's Cobble Hill neighborhood. With a bright and inviting atmosphere, a carefully curated selection of books, and frequent author events, it's a must-visit for book lovers.

Curiosity and facts: The store was opened in 2017 by author Emma Straub and her husband, Michael Fusco-Straub. They have a fantastic children's section and a great selection of signed books.

Getting there: Books Are Magic is located in the Cobble Hill neighborhood of Brooklyn, easily accessible by subway (F and G trains).

Nearby Attractions: The Brooklyn Bridge Park, the Barclays Center, and the Brooklyn Museum.

THE MYSTERIOUS BOOKSHOP

Address: 58 Warren St,
New York, NY 10007, United States.

Telephone: +1 212-587-1011.

Monday - Friday: 10:00 AM - 6:00 PM, Saturday: 11:00 AM - 5:00 PM, Sunday: Closed.

Tourist information: The Mysterious Bookshop specializes in crime fiction, thrillers, and mysteries. With a vast selection of new and rare titles, it's a must-visit for fans of the genre.

Curiosity and facts: The store was founded in 1979 and has been at its current location since 1995. They have a fantastic selection of signed first editions and a knowledgeable staff.

Getting there: The Mysterious Bookshop is located in the Tribeca neighborhood of Manhattan, easily accessible by subway (1, 2, 3, A, C, E, N, R, and W trains).

Nearby Attractions: The National September 11 Memorial & Museum, the Oculus, and Battery Park.

GREENLIGHT BOOKSTORE

Address: 686 Fulton St, Brooklyn, NY 11217, United States.

Telephone: +1 718-246-0200.

Monday - Sunday: 10:00 AM - 8:00 PM.

Tourist information: Greenlight Bookstore is an independent bookstore in the heart of Brooklyn's Fort Greene neighborhood. With a wide selection of new and classic titles, a knowledgeable staff, and frequent author events, it's a beloved community hub.

Curiosity and facts: Greenlight was founded in 2009 by two former editors, Rebecca Fitting and Jessica Stockton Bagnulo. They have a great selection of children's books and a popular book subscription service.

Getting there: Greenlight Bookstore is located in the Fort Greene neighborhood of Brooklyn, easily accessible by subway (C and G trains).

Nearby Attractions: The Brooklyn Academy of Music, Prospect Park, and the Brooklyn Botanic Garden.

HOUSING WORKS
BOOKSTORE CAFE

Address: 126 Crosby St,
New York, NY 10012, United States.

Telephone: +1 212-334-3324.

Monday - Sunday: 10:00 AM - 6:00 PM.

Tourist information: Housing Works Bookstore Cafe is a nonprofit bookstore in SoHo that supports the fight against AIDS and homelessness. With a cafe, events space, and a great selection of books, it's a fantastic place to shop and support a good cause.

Curiosity and facts: The store was founded in 1996 and has raised millions of dollars for Housing Works' programs. They have a fantastic selection of vintage and rare books and a bustling events calendar.

Getting there: Housing Works Bookstore Cafe is located in the SoHo neighborhood of Manhattan, easily accessible by subway (N, Q, R, W, 4, 6, and B, D, F, and M trains).

Nearby Attractions: The New Museum, The Drawing Center, and the iconic SoHo cast-iron buildings.

SHAKESPEARE & CO.

Address: 2020 Broadway,
New York, NY 10023, United States.

Telephone: +1 212-595-6859.

Monday - Sunday: 9:00 AM - 9:00 PM.

Tourist information: Shakespeare & Co. is a beloved independent bookstore on the Upper West Side. With a vast selection of books, a cozy atmosphere, and a cafe, it's a great place to spend an afternoon.

Curiosity and facts: The store was founded in 1981 and was named after the famous Parisian bookstore that served as a gathering place for writers such as Hemingway, Joyce, and Stein. They have a great selection of literary gifts and stationery.

Getting there: Shakespeare & Co. is located on the Upper West Side of Manhattan, easily accessible by subway (1, 2, 3, B, and C trains).

Nearby Attractions: The American Museum of Natural History, Central Park, and the Lincoln Center for the Performing Arts.

BLUESTOCKINGS

Address: 172 Allen St,
New York, NY 10002, United States.

Telephone: +1 212-777-6028.

Monday - Sunday: 12:00 PM - 8:00 PM.

Tourist information: Bluestockings is a radical bookstore and community center on the Lower East Side. With a focus on feminism, queer and gender studies, and social justice, it's a unique and important space.

Curiosity and facts: The store was founded in 1999 by a group of activists and has been volunteer-run ever since. They have a great selection of zines and independent publications and host a variety of events, including workshops and film screenings.

Getting there: Bluestockings is located on the Lower East Side of Manhattan, easily accessible by subway (F and M trains).

Nearby Attractions: The Tenement Museum, the New Museum, and the historic Essex Street Market.

RIZZOLI BOOKSTORE

Address: 1133 Broadway,
New York, NY 10010, United States.

Telephone: +1 212-759-2424.

Monday - Saturday: 10:00 AM - 7:00 PM, Sunday: 11:00 AM - 7:00 PM.

Tourist information: Rizzoli Bookstore is a beautiful and iconic bookstore in NoMad. With a focus on art, design, and architecture, it's a must-visit for anyone interested in these topics.

Curiosity and facts: The store was founded in 1964 and was originally located on Fifth Avenue. They have a great selection of coffee table books and a stunning interior with ornate details and a spiral staircase.

Getting there: Rizzoli Bookstore is located in the NoMad neighborhood of Manhattan, easily accessible by subway (R and W trains).

Nearby Attractions: The Flatiron Building, Madison Square Park, and the Museum of Sex.

ANTIQUE STORES

OLDE GOOD THINGS

Address: 333 W 52nd St, New York, NY 10019.

Telephone: (212) 675-3213.

Mon-Sat: 10am-7pm, Sun: 11am-6pm.

Tourist information: Olde Good Things is a vintage store that specializes in architectural salvage, antique tiles, and reclaimed wood. They have an extensive collection of unique and historic items, including doors, mantels, lighting, and hardware. Visitors can spend hours browsing through the store's many treasures.

Curiosity and facts: Olde Good Things has been featured on several TV shows, including "Salvage Dawgs" and "American Pickers." The company has also supplied materials for sets in movies such as "The Great Gatsby" and "Boardwalk Empire."

Getting there: Olde Good Things is located in the Hell's Kitchen neighborhood of Manhattan. The store is easily accessible by subway, with the C and E trains stopping nearby at 50th St. and 8th Ave.

Nearby attractions: Visitors to Olde Good Things can also check out nearby attractions such as the Intrepid Sea, Air & Space Museum and Times Square.

THE SHOWPLACE ANTIQUE & DESIGN CENTER

Address: 40 W 25th St,
New York, NY 10010.

Telephone: (212) 633-6063.

Mon-Fri: 10am-6pm, Sat-Sun: 8:30am-5:30pm.

Tourist information: The Showplace Antique & Design Center is a 4-story building that houses over 200 antique dealers. Visitors can find a wide variety of antiques and vintage items, including furniture, artwork, jewelry, and clothing. The center also hosts special events and exhibits throughout the year.

Curiosity and facts: The Showplace Antique & Design Center has been in business for over 25 years and is a favorite among antique enthusiasts and designers. The building itself is a landmark in the Flatiron District and features beautiful architectural details.

Getting there: The Showplace Antique & Design Center is located in the Flatiron District of Manhattan. The store is easily accessible by subway, with the R, W, and 6 trains stopping nearby at 23rd St.

Nearby attractions: Visitors to The Showplace Antique & Design Center can also check out nearby attractions such as Madison Square Park and the Flatiron Building.

NEW YORK VINTAGE

Address: 117 W 25th St,
New York, NY 10001.

Telephone: (212) 647-1107.

Mon-Sat: 11am-7pm, Sun: 12pm-6pm.

Tourist information: New York Vintage is a high-end vintage store that offers a curated selection of designer clothing, accessories, and jewelry from the 19th and 20th centuries. Visitors can find pieces from iconic fashion houses such as Chanel, Yves Saint Laurent, and Christian Dior.

Curiosity and facts: New York Vintage has been featured in numerous fashion magazines and is a go-to destination for stylists and celebrities. The store has also collaborated with designers such as Marc Jacobs and has loaned pieces for movie and TV productions.

Getting there: New York Vintage is located in the Chelsea neighborhood of Manhattan. The store is easily accessible by subway, with the F and M trains stopping nearby at 23rd St. and 6th Ave.

Nearby attractions: Visitors to New York Vintage can also check out nearby attractions such as the High Line and the Rubin Museum of Art.

JOHN DERIAN COMPANY

Address: 6 E 2nd St,
New York, NY 10003.

Telephone: (212) 677-3917.

Mon-Sat: 11am-7pm, Sun: 12pm-6pm.

Tourist information: John Derian Company is a home decor store that specializes in decoupage. Visitors can find a variety of unique and whimsical items such as trays, paperweights, and plates that are decorated with vintage images and botanical prints.

Curiosity and facts: John Derian Company has been in business for over 30 years and is a favorite among interior designers and collectors. The store's products have been featured in magazines such as Elle Decor and House Beautiful.

Getting there: John Derian Company is located in the East Village neighborhood of Manhattan. The store is easily accessible by subway, with the F train stopping nearby at 2nd Ave.

Nearby attractions: Visitors to John Derian Company can also check out nearby attractions such as Tompkins Square Park and the Tenement Museum.

ALAN MOSS STUDIOS

Address: 73 Spring St,
New York, NY 10012.

Telephone: (212) 343-2288.

By appointment only.

Tourist information: Alan Moss Studios is an art gallery that specializes in contemporary glass art. Visitors can find a variety of unique and beautiful pieces, including vases, sculptures, and chandeliers.

Curiosity and facts: Alan Moss Studios has been in business for over 20 years and is a leading authority in the world of glass art. The gallery's artists have won numerous awards and have exhibited their work in museums and galleries around the world.

Getting there: Alan Moss Studios is located in the SoHo neighborhood of Manhattan. The gallery is easily accessible by subway, with the 6 train stopping nearby at Spring St.

Nearby attractions: Visitors to Alan Moss Studios can also check out nearby attractions such as the New York City Fire Museum and the Leslie-Lohman Museum of Art.

THE ANTIQUE AND ARTISAN GALLERY

Address: 69 Jefferson St,
Stamford, CT 06902.

Telephone: (203) 327-6022.

Mon-Sat: 10am-5pm, Sun: 12pm-5pm.

Tourist information: The Antique and Artisan Gallery is a multi-dealer antique store located just outside of New York City in Stamford, CT. Visitors can find a variety of antique and vintage items, including furniture, artwork, and jewelry.

Curiosity and facts: The Antique and Artisan Gallery has been in business for over 30 years and has a reputation for offering high-quality antiques at fair prices. The store's dealers are knowledgeable and passionate about their collections.

Getting there: The Antique and Artisan Gallery is located in Stamford, CT, just a short train ride from New York City. Visitors can take the Metro-North New Haven line from Grand Central Terminal to Stamford Station.

Nearby attractions: Visitors to The Antique and Artisan Gallery can also check out nearby attractions such as the Stamford Museum and Nature Center and the Stamford Downtown Farmers Market.

FURNISH GREEN

Address: 1261 Broadway #309, New York, NY 10001.

Telephone: (917) 583-9051.

Mon-Fri: 10am-8pm, Sat-Sun: 10am-6pm.

Tourist information: Furnish Green is a vintage furniture store that offers a mix of mid-century modern, industrial, and antique pieces. Visitors can find everything from sofas and tables to lamps and wall art.

Curiosity and facts: Furnish Green is committed to sustainability and offers a variety of eco-friendly and upcycled products. The store has also been featured in numerous media outlets, including The New York Times and Architectural Digest.

Getting there: Furnish Green is located in the NoMad neighborhood of Manhattan. The store is easily accessible by subway, with the

N, Q, R, and W trains stopping nearby at 34th St. and Herald Square.

Nearby attractions: Visitors to Furnish Green can also check out nearby attractions such as the Empire State Building and the Morgan Library & Museum.

BILLY'S ANTIQUES & PROPS

Address: 76 E Houston St,
New York, NY 10012.

Telephone: (212) 260-9362.

Mon-Sun: 11am-7pm.

Tourist information: Billy's Antiques & Props is a unique store that specializes in vintage and eclectic items. Visitors can find a variety of oddities and curiosities, including taxidermy, vintage signs, and antique furniture.

Curiosity and facts: Billy's Antiques & Props has been in business for over 30 years and is a favorite among film and TV production companies. The store's items have been used in movies such as "The Devil Wears Prada" and "Sex and the City."

Getting there: Billy's Antiques & Props is located in the NoLIta neighborhood of Manhattan. The store is easily accessible by subway, with the 6 train stopping nearby at Spring St.

Nearby attractions: Visitors to Billy's Antiques & Props can also check out nearby attractions such as the New Museum and the Bowery Ballroom.

NAGA ANTIQUES

Address: 403 E 73rd St,
New York, NY 10021.

Telephone: (212) 517-9623.

Mon-Sat: 10am-5pm.

Tourist information: Naga Antiques is a high-end antique store that specializes in Asian art and antiques. Visitors can find a variety of rare and unique pieces, including ceramics, sculptures, and furniture.

Curiosity and facts: Naga Antiques has been in business for over 25 years and has a reputation for offering museum-quality pieces. The store's owner, Sherle Wagner, is a noted collector and expert in Asian art and antiques.

Getting there: Naga Antiques is located on the Upper East Side of Manhattan. The store is easily accessible by subway, with the 6 train stopping nearby at 68th St. and Lexington Ave.

Nearby attractions: Visitors to Naga Antiques can also check out nearby attractions such as the Metropolitan Museum of Art and Central Park.

THE END OF HISTORY

Address: 548 Laguardia Pl,
New York, NY 10012.

Telephone: (212) 647-7598.

Mon-Sat: 11am-7pm, Sun: 12pm-6pm.

Tourist information: The End of History is a home decor store that specializes in vintage and modern glassware. Visitors can find a variety of unique and beautiful pieces, including vases, bowls, and decanters.

Curiosity and facts: The End of History has been in business for over 20 years and has a reputation for offering rare and collectible glassware. The store's owner, Peter West, is a glass artist and curator who has exhibited his work in museums and galleries around the world.

Getting there: The End of History is located in the Greenwich Village neighborhood of Manhattan. The store is easily accessible by subway, with the A, B, C, D, E, F, and M trains stopping nearby at West 4th St.

Nearby attractions: Visitors to The End of History can also check out nearby attractions such as Washington Square Park and the New York University campus.

ART GALLERIES STORES

THE MUSEUM OF MODERN ART

Address: 11 West 53 Street,
New York, NY 10019.

Telephone: +1 (212) 708-9400.

Sunday to Thursday from 10:30 AM to 5:30 PM, Friday and Saturday from 10:30 AM to 9:00 PM.

Tourist information: The Museum of Modern Art houses a vast collection of modern and contemporary art, including works by famous artists such as Vincent van Gogh, Pablo Picasso, and Andy Warhol. Visitors can also enjoy temporary exhibitions, film screenings, and educational programs.

Curiosity and facts: The Museum of Modern Art was the first museum dedicated entirely to modern art in the United States, opening in 1929. The museum's collection includes more than 200,000 works of art and design.

Getting there: The Museum of Modern Art is located in Midtown Manhattan, near the corner of 53rd Street and Fifth Avenue. Visitors can take the subway to the Fifth

Avenue/53rd Street station, which is served by the E and M trains.

Nearby attractions: Central Park, Rockefeller Center, St. Patrick's Cathedral, and the Museum of Arts and Design.

GAGOSIAN GALLERY

Address: 555 West 24th Street,
New York, NY 10011.

Telephone: +1 (212) 741-1111.

Tuesday to Saturday from 10:00 AM to 6:00 PM.

Tourist information: The Gagosian Gallery is one of the world's leading contemporary art galleries, representing a roster of influential artists such as Jeff Koons, Richard Serra, and Takashi Murakami. Visitors can view exhibitions of painting, sculpture, photography, and other media.

Curiosity and facts: The Gagosian Gallery was founded by Larry Gagosian in 1980 and has since expanded to 16 locations worldwide, including galleries in London, Paris, Hong Kong, and Beverly Hills.

Getting there: The Gagosian Gallery is located in the Chelsea neighborhood of Manhattan, near the corner of 11th Avenue and 24th Street. Visitors can take the subway to the 23rd Street station, which is served by the C and E trains.

Nearby attractions: The High Line, Chelsea Market, Chelsea Piers, and the Rubin Museum of Art.

DAVID ZWIRNER GALLERY

Address: 537 West 20th Street, New York, NY 10011.

Telephone: +1 (212) 517-8677.

Tuesday to Saturday from 10:00 AM to 6:00 PM.

Tourist information: The David Zwirner Gallery is a contemporary art gallery with locations in New York, London, and Hong Kong. The gallery represents a diverse range of artists, including Yayoi Kusama, Chris Ofili, and Kerry James Marshall.

Curiosity and facts: David Zwirner opened his first gallery in 1993 in SoHo and has since become one of the most influential figures in the contemporary art world. In 2012, the gallery moved to its current location in Chelsea, which features five floors of exhibition space.

Getting there: The David Zwirner Gallery is located in the Chelsea neighborhood of Manhattan, near the corner of 20th Street and

11th Avenue. Visitors can take the subway to the 23rd Street station, which is served by the C and E trains.

Nearby attractions: The High Line, Chelsea Market, Chelsea Piers, and the Rubin Museum of Art.

PACE GALLERY

Address: 540 West 25th Street,
New York, NY 10001.

Telephone: +1 (212) 989-4258.

Tuesday to Saturday from 10:00 AM to 6:00 PM.

Tourist information: The Pace Gallery is a contemporary art gallery with locations in New York, London, Beijing, and Hong Kong. The gallery represents a diverse range of artists, including Chuck Close, Robert Rauschenberg, and Maya Lin.

Curiosity and facts: The Pace Gallery was founded by Arne Glimcher in 1960 and has since become one of the most respected galleries in the world. In addition to its exhibition program, the gallery also publishes catalogs and books on modern and contemporary art.

Getting there: The Pace Gallery is located in the Chelsea neighborhood of Manhattan, near the corner of 25th Street and 11th Avenue. Visitors can take the subway to the 23rd Street station, which is served by the C and E trains.

Nearby attractions: The High Line, Chelsea Market, Chelsea Piers, and the Rubin Museum of Art.

HAUSER & WIRTH

Address: 548 West 22nd Street, New York, NY 10011.

Telephone: +1 (212) 790-3900.

Tuesday to Saturday from 10:00 AM to 6:00 PM.

Tourist information: Hauser & Wirth is a contemporary art gallery with locations in New York, Los Angeles, London, Somerset, Zurich, and Hong Kong. The gallery represents a diverse range of artists, including Louise Bourgeois, Mark Bradford, and Paul McCarthy.

Curiosity and facts: Hauser & Wirth was founded in 1992 by Iwan and Manuela Wirth and Ursula Hauser and has since become one of the leading contemporary art galleries in the world. The gallery is known for its support of emerging artists and its commitment to fostering cultural dialogue.

Getting there: Hauser & Wirth is located in the Chelsea neighborhood of Manhattan, near the corner of 22nd Street and 11th Avenue. Visitors can take the subway to the 23rd Street station, which is served by the C and E trains.

Nearby attractions: The High Line, Chelsea Market, Chelsea Piers, and the Rubin Museum of Art.

THE METROPOLITAN MUSEUM OF ART STORE

Address: 1000 Fifth Avenue, New York, NY 10028.

Telephone: +1 (212) 570-3894.

Sunday to Thursday from 10:00 AM to 5:30 PM, Friday and Saturday from 10:00 AM to 9:00 PM.

Tourist information: The Metropolitan Museum of Art Store offers a wide selection of art-inspired gifts, books, jewelry, and home decor, as well as reproductions of works from the museum's collection. Visitors can also purchase tickets for exhibitions and events.

Curiosity and facts: The Metropolitan Museum of Art was founded in 1870 and is one of the largest and most comprehensive art museums in the world, with a collection of over two million works of art. The museum's collection spans 5,000 years of world culture and includes objects from ancient Egypt, Europe, Asia, and the Americas.

Getting there: The Metropolitan Museum of Art is located on Fifth Avenue in the Upper East Side of Manhattan. Visitors can take the subway to the 86th Street station, which is served by the 4, 5, and 6 trains.

Nearby attractions: Central Park, The Frick Collection, The Guggenheim Museum, and The Cooper Hewitt Smithsonian Design Museum.

THE WHITNEY MUSEUM OF AMERICAN ART STORE

Address: 99 Gansevoort Street,
New York, NY 10014.

Telephone: +1 (212) 570-3600.

Monday and Wednesday to Thursday from 10:30 AM to 6:00 PM, Friday from 10:30 AM to 10:00 PM, Saturday and Sunday from 10:30 AM to 6:00 PM.

Tourist information: The Whitney Museum of American Art Store offers a variety of art-inspired gifts, books, jewelry, and home decor, as well as reproductions of works from the museum's collection. Visitors can also purchase tickets for exhibitions and events.

Curiosity and facts: The Whitney Museum of American Art was founded in 1930 by Gertrude Vanderbilt Whitney and is dedicated to collecting, preserving, interpreting, and exhibiting American art. The museum's collection includes more than 23,000 works by over 3,500 artists, including Edward Hopper, Georgia O'Keeffe, and Andy Warhol.

Getting there: The Whitney Museum of American Art is located in the Meatpacking District of Manhattan, near the corner of Gansevoort Street and Washington Street. Visitors can take the subway to the 14th Street station, which is served by the A, C, E, and L trains.

Nearby attractions: The High Line, The Chelsea Market, The Rubin Museum of Art, and The Museum at FIT.

THE NEW MUSEUM STORE

Address: 235 Bowery,
New York, NY 10002.

Telephone: +1 (212) 219-1222.

Wednesday to Sunday from 11:00 AM to 6:00 PM, Thursday from 11:00 AM to 9:00 PM.

Tourist information: The New Museum Store offers a unique selection of art books, prints, and limited-edition works by contemporary artists, as well as gifts and souvenirs related to the museum's exhibitions and programming.

Curiosity and facts: The New Museum was founded in 1977 and is dedicated to promoting new ideas and approaches in contemporary art. The museum has a reputation for showcasing emerging artists and supporting experimental projects and exhibitions.

Getting there: The New Museum is located on Bowery in the Lower East Side of Manhattan, near the corner of Prince Street. Visitors can take the subway to the Second Avenue station, which is served by the F train.

Nearby attractions: The Tenement Museum, The Museum of Chinese in America, The Bowery Ballroom, and The Lower East Side Tenement Museum.

LEHMANN MAUPIN GALLERY

Address: 501 West 24th Street, New York, NY 10011.

Telephone: +1 (212) 255-2923.

Tuesday to Saturday from 10:00 AM to 6:00 PM.

Tourist information: Lehmann Maupin Gallery is a contemporary art gallery with locations in New York, Hong Kong, and Seoul. The gallery represents a diverse range of artists, including Teresita Fernández, Nari Ward, and Gilbert & George.

Curiosity and facts: Lehmann Maupin Gallery was founded in 1996 by Rachel Lehmann and David Maupin and has since become one of the most respected galleries in the contemporary art world. The gallery is known for its commitment to fostering new and experimental work by both emerging and established artists.

Getting there: Lehmann Maupin Gallery is located in the Chelsea neighborhood of Manhattan, near the corner of 24th Street and 10th Avenue. Visitors can take the subway to the 23rd Street station, which is served by the C and E trains.

Nearby attractions: The High Line, Chelsea Market, Chelsea Piers, and the Rubin Museum of Art.

SEAN KELLY GALLERY

Address: 475 Tenth Avenue,
New York, NY 10018.

Telephone: +1 (212) 239-1181.

Tuesday to Saturday from 11:00 AM to 6:00 PM.

Tourist information: Sean Kelly Gallery is a contemporary art gallery with locations in New York and Taipei. The gallery represents a diverse range of artists, including Marina Abramović, Antony Gormley, and Sam Moyer.

Curiosity and facts: Sean Kelly Gallery was founded in 1991 and has since become one of the most influential galleries in the contemporary art world. The gallery is known for its innovative exhibitions and its commitment to supporting emerging and mid-career artists.

Getting there: Sean Kelly Gallery is located in the Hell's Kitchen neighborhood of Manhattan, near the corner of 36th Street and 10th Avenue. Visitors can take the subway to the 34th Street-Hudson Yards station, which is served by the 7 train.

Nearby attractions: The Javits Center, The Intrepid Sea, Air & Space Museum, The Vessel at Hudson Yards, and The High Line.

STREET MARKETS STORES

CHELSEA MARKET

Address: 75 9th Ave,
New York, NY 10011.

Telephone: (212) 652-2110.

Monday-Saturday 7am-10pm, Sunday 8am-9pm.

Tourist information: The Chelsea Market is a food hall with over 35 vendors, including seafood, bakeries, cafes, and restaurants. The market is a popular destination for tourists and locals alike.

Curiosity and facts: The Chelsea Market is housed in the former National Biscuit Company (Nabisco) factory, where the Oreo cookie was invented.

Getting there: The market is located in the Chelsea neighborhood, easily accessible by public transportation, including the A, C, E, and L subway lines.

Nearby attractions: The High Line, Chelsea Piers, and the Whitney Museum of American

Art are all within walking distance of the market.

SMORGASBURG

Address: East River State Park, 90 Kent Ave, Brooklyn, NY 11211.

Telephone: (718) 928-6603.

Saturdays 11am-6pm (April-October); Sundays 11am-5pm (April-November).

Tourist information: Smorgasburg is a popular outdoor food market featuring over 100 local and regional food vendors. The market attracts both locals and tourists, with options ranging from artisanal ice cream to sushi burritos.

Curiosity and facts: Smorgasburg was started in 2011 as a spinoff of the Brooklyn Flea, another popular outdoor market in New York City.

Getting there: The market is located in Williamsburg, Brooklyn, and is accessible by subway (L train to Bedford Ave or the East River Ferry).

Nearby attractions: The market is located in East River State Park, which offers stunning views of the Manhattan skyline. Visitors can also explore the trendy Williamsburg neighborhood and nearby shops and boutiques.

UNION SQUARE GREENMARKET

Address: Union Square Park, New York, NY 10003.

Telephone: (212) 788-7476.

Mondays, Wednesdays, Fridays, and Saturdays 8am-6pm (April-November); Mondays, Wednesdays, and Saturdays 8am-4pm (December-March).

Tourist information: The Union Square Greenmarket is a farmer's market featuring locally grown produce and artisanal goods. Visitors can browse stalls selling fresh fruits and vegetables, baked goods, and handmade cheeses.

Curiosity and facts: The Union Square Greenmarket was founded in 1976 and has since become a staple of the New York City food scene.

Getting there: The market is located in Union Square Park and is easily accessible by public transportation, including several subway lines and bus routes.

Nearby attractions: Union Square is a bustling neighborhood with plenty of shops, restaurants, and cafes to explore. The park itself is also a popular spot for picnics and outdoor gatherings.

ESSEX MARKET

Address: 88 Essex St, New York, NY 10002.

Telephone: (212) 312-3603.

Monday-Saturday 8am-8pm, Sunday 10am-6pm.

Tourist information: The Essex Market is a historic indoor market featuring over 30 vendors selling a variety of foods, including fresh produce, artisanal cheeses, and baked goods. The market is a popular destination for foodies and visitors looking to explore the Lower East Side.

Curiosity and facts: The Essex Market dates back to the 1940s and was recently renovated to include a new location on the Lower East Side.

Getting there: The market is located on the Lower East Side and is accessible by several subway lines and bus routes.

Nearby attractions: Visitors can explore the Lower East Side, including nearby shops, restaurants, and cultural landmarks such as the Tenement Museum.

THE BROOKLYN FLEA

Address: 80 Pearl St,
Brooklyn, NY 11201.

Telephone: (718) 928-6603.

Saturdays and Sundays 10am-6pm.

Tourist information: The Brooklyn Flea is a popular outdoor market featuring vintage clothing, antiques, and artisanal food vendors. Visitors can browse over 100 stalls and sample a variety of foods, from homemade ice cream to wood-fired pizza.

Curiosity and facts: The Brooklyn Flea was founded in 2008 and has since become a popular destination for vintage and handmade goods in New York City.

Getting there: The market has multiple locations, but the Pearl Street location is accessible by subway (A, C, F, and R trains to Jay St-MetroTech).

Nearby attractions: Visitors can explore the trendy DUMBO neighborhood and nearby Brooklyn Bridge Park, which offers stunning views of the Manhattan skyline.

GRAND BAZAAR NYC

Address: 100 W 77th St,
New York, NY 10024.

Telephone: (212) 239-3025.

Sundays 10am-5:30pm.

Tourist information: The Grand Bazaar NYC is a weekly indoor and outdoor market featuring over 100 vendors selling a variety of goods, including vintage clothing, handmade jewelry, and artisanal foods. The market is a popular destination for both locals and tourists.

Curiosity and facts: The Grand Bazaar NYC is the largest weekly market in New York City, and a portion of the proceeds go to benefit local public schools.

Getting there: The market is located on the Upper West Side and is accessible by subway (1 train to 79th St).

Nearby attractions: Visitors can explore the nearby American Museum of Natural History or Central Park.

HELL'S KITCHEN FLEA MARKET

Address: West 39th St, between 9th and 10th Ave, New York, NY 10018.

Telephone: (212) 243-5343.

Saturdays and Sundays 9am-5pm.

Tourist information: The Hell's Kitchen Flea Market is a popular outdoor market featuring vintage clothing, antiques, and handmade goods. Visitors can browse over 100 stalls and find unique and one-of-a-kind items.

Curiosity and facts: The market is located in the historic Hell's Kitchen neighborhood, known for its restaurants and nightlife.

Getting there: The market is accessible by subway (A, C, E, N, Q, R, and W trains to 42nd St-Times Square).

Nearby attractions: Visitors can explore the nearby Theater District or Times Square.

GANSEVOORT MARKET

Address: 353 W 14th St,
New York, NY 10014.

Telephone: (212) 929-5900.

Daily 8am-9pm.

Tourist information: The Gansevoort Market is an indoor food hall featuring a variety of vendors, including a raw bar, gourmet sandwiches, and artisanal desserts. The market is a popular destination for foodies and visitors looking to explore the Meatpacking District.

Curiosity and facts: The market is located in a historic building that dates back to the 1800s, and was once a prominent spot for farmers to sell their goods in the city.

Getting there: The market is located in the Meatpacking District and is accessible by subway (A, C, E, and L trains to 14th St).

Nearby attractions: Visitors can explore the nearby High Line park or the Whitney Museum of American Art.

WASHINGTON SQUARE OUTDOOR ART EXHIBIT

Address: Washington Square Park, New York, NY 10012.

Telephone: (212) 982-6255.

Memorial Day Weekend and Labor Day Weekend, 12pm-6pm.

Tourist information: The Washington Square Outdoor Art Exhibit is a bi-annual outdoor art show featuring works by local and national artists. Visitors can browse a variety of art, including paintings, sculptures, and photographs.

Curiosity and facts: The exhibit has been held in Washington Square Park since 1931 and is a longstanding tradition in New York City's art scene.

Getting there: The exhibit is located in Washington Square Park and is accessible by subway (A, B, C, D, E, F, and M trains to West 4th St).

Nearby attractions: Visitors can explore the nearby Greenwich Village neighborhood, including the historic Stonewall Inn and nearby cafes and restaurants.

ARTISTS & FLEAS

Address: 568 Broadway,
New York, NY 10012.

Telephone: (917) 488-0044.

Daily 11am-8pm.

Tourist information: Artists & Fleas is an indoor market featuring over 30 vendors selling a variety of handmade goods, including jewelry, clothing, and home decor. The market is a popular destination for visitors looking for unique and one-of-a-kind items.

Curiosity and facts: The market began in 2003 in Williamsburg, Brooklyn and has since expanded to include multiple locations in New York City.

Getting there: The market is located in SoHo and is accessible by subway (N, Q, R, W, 4, 5, and 6 trains to Canal St).

Nearby attractions: Visitors can explore the nearby SoHo neighborhood, including boutique shops, art galleries, and cafes.

Printed in Great Britain
by Amazon